FEARLESS WARRIORS

NINJAS

Rupert
Matthews

W
FRANKLIN WATTS
LONDON · SYDNEY

Franklin Watts

First published in Great Britain in 2016 by The Watts Publishing Group

Copyright © Alix Wood Books
Produced for Franklin Watts by Alix Wood Books **www.alixwoodbooks.co.uk**

Editor: Eloise Macgregor
Designer: Alix Wood

Photo Credits:
Cover, 1, 3, 4 top, 6, 8, 9, 12, 13 bottom, 15, 18 top, 21, 24, 25 top, 30, 31 bottom, 32 bottom, 33 top and middle, 37 top © Shutterstock; 4 bottom © Timitzer; 7 main image © Alpsdake; 11, 33 bottom © Samuraiantiqueworld; 13 top, 29 top © Dollar Photo Club; 14 © Trustees of the British Museum; 20 © Howard Smith; 25 bottom © biwako; 31 top © Zach Toups; 38 © Maha Vajra; 43 © specialoperations; remaining images are in the public domain

ISBN 978 1 4451 5051 2

Printed in China

Franklin Watts
An imprint of
Hachette Children's Group
Part of The Watts Publishing Group
Carmelite House
50 Victoria Embankment
London EC4Y 0DZ

An Hachette UK Company

www.hachette.co.uk
www.franklinwatts.co.uk

MIX
Paper from
responsible sources
FSC® C104740
FSC
www.fsc.org

Contents

Secret killers

He stood still in the shadows. Very still. Footsteps approached, and he held his breath. First two guards, then the **warlord**. He quickly threw two **shuriken**, which brushed the guards' necks as if a fly had flown by. As they looked away, he stepped forward and touched the warlord lightly with the secret death touch. He melted back into the shadows. Nobody had seen him. The warlord and guards walked on. In an hour the warlord would be dead!

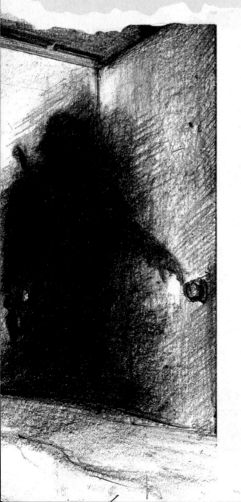

Those who worked as ninja called themselves **shinobi**, a word which means 'the hidden one'. The shinobi moved through the shadows of the night dressed in black, or they disguised themselves as harmless peasants to evade guards or those who hunted them. It was said that nobody could see a ninja, unless the ninja wanted to be seen.

a shuriken

Since they were so secretive about what they did and how they did it, the history of the ninja is often vague. We know that they were most active during the Sengoku period of Japanese history. This period lasted from about 1450 to 1603 and was a time of **civil war**, rebellions and warlords. The constant conflicts provided lots of job opportunities for experts in stealth warfare!

That's fearless!

Ninja Jiraiya owned a large collection of pet toads. He is said to have sent the toads to creep into the houses and castles of enemies to spy for him. In legends about Jiraiya he is able to turn himself into a giant toad!

OUT OF WORK

When peace came to Japan under the powerful Tokugawa **shoguns** in 1603 the job opportunities for ninja fell. As their numbers dwindled in real life, the ninja became more and more popular in legends. All sorts of books, plays and tales about the ninja became common. It can be difficult now to tell what is the truth and what is a legend when we read about the ninja.

The ninja Jiraiya riding a giant toad

Ninja clans

True ninja came from a small number of **samurai** clans in remote mountain valleys. They perfected the skills that made the ninja so feared and admired throughout Japan.

From earliest times Japanese nobles used spies and secret agents. These men went in disguise, crept into enemy camps, and tried to murder enemy leaders. However, these men were not ninja, they were ordinary soldiers. They often failed in their missions. It was the fact that ordinary soldiers failed so often that led to the rise of the ninja.

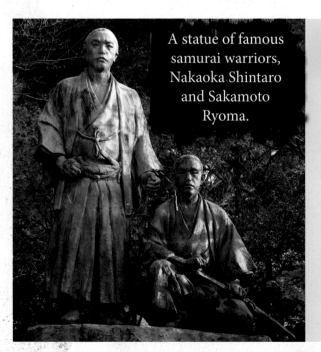

A statue of famous samurai warriors, Nakaoka Shintaro and Sakamoto Ryoma.

SAMURAI PRIDE

The key fighting men of Japan were the samurai. This class of noble warrior believed in a strict code of honour. The code demanded that they fight their enemies openly with weapons that needed skill to use properly. The samurai were too proud to act as spies or **assassins**, so the nobles had to find others who would.

In around 1300, in the steep mountains to the south of the island of Honshu, were the remote valleys of the Iga and Koga regions. There were no roads into the valleys, only narrow and winding footpaths. The Iga and Koga people decided to refuse to pay taxes or send **tributes** to the emperor or nearby lords. These families were not noble samurai but farmers and hunters. To keep their freedom, the clans of Iga and Koga became ninja.

a hunter

The men were organised into ninja clans. Each clan was led by a man with the title of **jonin**. He organised training, discipline and finances. Each clan had a number of **chunin** who organised missions and negotiated how much the clan would be paid. Some clans hired themselves out for individual tasks, others worked for a single lord for many years. The **genin** were the men who actually carried out ninja missions.

Mountains in the Iga region of Japan

Ninja training

Ninja trained throughout their lives. If they were wounded or too old to be ninja, they were still useful. Retired ninja thought up ideas and techniques to pass on to the younger men to use in action.

Ninja started training at the age of about five years. At first a boy would be trained in all aspects of ninja, but by the age of about 10 he would begin to specialise. Emphasis would be put on whatever skills the boy was best at. By the time he was ready to go into action, at the age of about 16, he would be a master of at least one type of ninja task.

Ninja were trained to use plants to make medicines or poisons. A famous ninja medicine was the 'black potion', which stopped bleeding and prevented wounds from becoming infected.

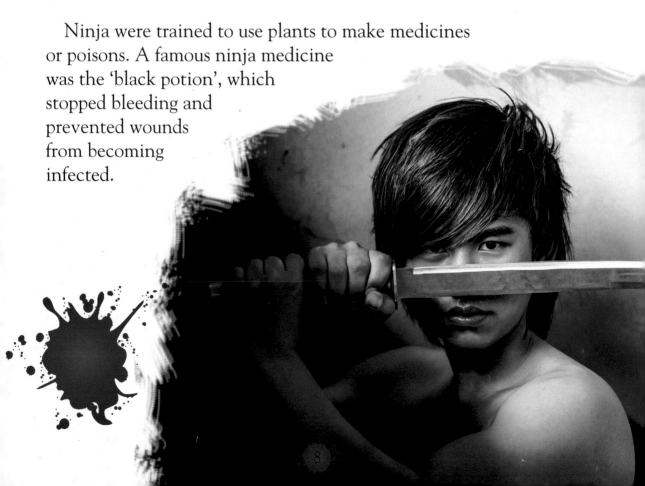

Ninja often wore a disguise when on a mission. Because of this they were trained in many skills so that they could convince people they were who they were pretending to be. If they were pretending to be a monk they needed to know prayers and songs. If they were disguised as a cook they learned how to prepare meals. Pretend entertainers learned how to sing, or how to juggle.

That's fearless!

Ninja trained doing long-distance runs. The runs were usually through the mountains and would go up steep hills and cliffs!

STEALTH TRAINING

Ninja were trained to walk over the ground without leaving footprints and how to swim without causing a splash or ripple on the water's surface.

The ninja believed that the positions of the stars and planets had a great influence on human affairs. Ninja trained in the art of **astrology**. They learned the meanings of different star positions and events such as shooting stars or comets. Before going on a mission the ninja would consult the stars to decide the best methods to use.

The oniwaban

In 1581 the Iga mountains were conquered by the warlord Oda Nobunaga after a long war. The ninja clans were no longer their own boss. Instead of hiring their services out to whoever they wanted, the ninja became the servants of the warlords.

The Tensho Iga war

In 1576 Oda Nobunaga conquered the Ise Province. In theory this should have given him control of the Iga clans, but it did not. In 1579 Nobunaga's son Nobukatsu led an invasion of Iga. His army was heavily defeated by the ninja clans using ambush and other ninja tactics. In 1581 Nobunaga invaded with a large army. The ninja scattered from Iga to take service with other lords.

A statue of Oda Nobunaga in Gifu, Japan

In 1684 the shogun declared it illegal for anyone other than himself to have ninja! He formed the ninja into a secret service, the 'oniwaban'. Oniwaban means 'garden guards'. The twenty oniwaban controlled a large number of men, all trained in some ninja techniques. They kept watch on nobles on behalf of the shogun, and guarded the shogun himself. The oniwaban were disbanded when the **shogunate** was abolished in 1868.

The 18 skills

By around 1700, ninja training schools were teaching 'the 18 skills'. These skills were:

1. spiritual skills
2. unarmed combat
3. sword fighting
4. fighting using sticks
5. fighting with spears
6. fighting using a **naginata**
7. fighting using a **kusarigama**
8. throwing bladed weapons
9. using fire and explosives
10. disguise and impersonation
11. stealth and entering
12. horsemanship
13. stealth and combat on water
14. battle tactics
15. spying techniques
16. escaping and hiding
17. weather forecasting
18. geography

a naginata

a kusarigama

That's fearless!

In 1858 men of the oniwaban even travelled to the US. They went to spy on the shogun's enemies and to discover the true strength of America.

Spying

The most important job of the ninja was to enter enemy territory to spy and gather information. Their ability to know what was going on all over Japan made them feared and respected.

Secrecy was vital. If a noble, or **daimyo**, wanted to spy on a rival he would hire the ninja. The ninja would ask what they needed to find out and agree a price. The ninja never revealed how they got the information.

The rich, powerful daimyo wore fine clothes.

The ninja sometimes lied about their methods. They may say they used kites to scout out the land. Or they might say they could talk to animals, such as rats or birds and send animals into a rival's home to get information. Some daimyos made huge efforts to stop animals getting into their homes, thinking that it would stop the ninja learning their secrets! These stories helped cover up their real techniques.

Master spy Nakagawa Shoshujin used all sorts of ninja techniques to find out the secrets of Japanese daimyos. When asked how he did it, he said he turned himself into a bird and flew around Japan listening to what people were saying.

That's fearless!

Before the siege of Hara Castle in 1637 ninja Ukai Kanemon learned the sentries' password. Throughout the siege Kanemon entered the castle each night using the password to spy on the defenders.

HIDDEN MIST

The name of the ninja Kirigakure Saizo means 'hidden mist'. He probably got this name from his skills at hiding and camouflage. In his most famous exploit he was sent to spy on the samurai daimyo Toyotomi Hideyoshi. Saizo hid under the floorboards of Hideyoshi's house, squirming silently from room to room eavesdropping! According to one story he saved Hideyoshi's life by appearing out of the floorboards to stop a treacherous samurai from murdering him!

Most daimyo did not have much money. They owned farms, had armies of samurai, and lived in luxurious homes, but all this was given to them in return for favours. The only money in use in Japan was old Chinese coins. After 1601, Japanese coins were made, but these were mostly used by the government. Daimyos hiring ninja usually paid in sacks of rice!

Sabotage

Entering enemy territory and damaging their weapons or property is known as sabotage. Ninja would be sent into camps to sabotage items useful to the enemy forces. Ninja techniques meant they could do their work and then leave without anyone knowing they had been there. Often the damage was put down to accidents or mistakes, not to the ninja.

In 1541 the great castle at Kasagi was under siege. The attackers hired ninja to destroy the food stores inside. The ninja secretly entered the castle and set fire to the storerooms, some living quarters, and other buildings. The defenders were starved into surrender soon after. This was the second time that ninja had burned Kasagi! In 1331 they burned down a temple there to keep it from being used as a military supply base.

During the 1331 siege of Kasagi Castle, the temple was raided in the night by attackers who climbed the cliffs and set it alight.

In 1558 a group of 49 ninja used what they called the 'ghost technique' to enter and destroy Sawayama Castle. This technique involved quietly entering a building by pretending that they were supposed to be there. They stole a lantern used by a sentry that was decorated with the family emblem. They made 49 identical lanterns and used these to pretend to be returning sentries. Having entered the castle the ninja set fire to dozens of buildings. This allowed their employer, Rokkaku Yoshitaka, to launch an attack and capture the castle.

STUBBORN NINJA

When warlord Kizawa Nagamasa hired three senior ninja he found they would not do what he asked. He hired the elite ninja to set fire to Maibara Castle, which he was attacking, telling them exactly which buildings to set on fire and when to do so. The ninja refused, saying that they would decide when to begin the fires. Nagamasa backed down and told the ninja to do what they thought best. A few nights later the fires broke out and Nagamasa captured Maibara.

Assassination

The proud samurai lords and daimyo of Japan believed that it was honourable to face their enemies in open battle and a fair fight. The ninja thought that any method of getting rid of an enemy was acceptable. A secret killing was effective, but rarely simple.

Kumawaka escaping by swinging on a bamboo plant

Ninja Kumawaka wanted to kill the samurai Saburo, as he had ordered his father's execution. He got into Saburo's house and spent the next five nights creeping about the house to plan the killing. On the final night he opened a door and moths flew into the lantern flames. The lanterns went out and plunged the house into darkness. Kumawaka crept into Saburo's bedroom and killed him with his own sword. Kumawaka then climbed a tall bamboo plant so that it bent over and landed him on the far side of a stream. When the alarm was raised Kumawaka was already far away!

Uesugi Kenshin's ninja assassin realised he was only unguarded when Kenshin went to the bathroom. The ninja crept under the toilet seat and waited. When Kenshin appeared the ninja stabbed him with a short spear and got away.

Warlord Uesugi Kenshin

Some ninja were said to kill using the 'touch of death'. By pushing his fingers into a point on the victim's body one of their organs would stop working. Death happened hours or days later. Nobody is sure if this technique really worked, or if it was just another ninja cover story!

Ninja Hachisuka Tenzo was an expert shot. He was sent to kill the warlord Takeda Shingen. At his first attempt he hid in a hole in a tree, shot, and missed. Shingen's guards could not find him. That night Tenzo crept to where Shingen was sleeping. It was a cloudy, pitch black night. Despite this, Tenzo spotted which sleeping man was Shingen, and shot him dead from outside the camp, before sneaking away.

NIGHTINGALE FLOORS

To try to stop ninja creeping around, some samurai lords used special noisy floors, called 'nightingale floors'. The floorboards would be slightly raised so that if a person trod on them they bent downwards. Under the floorboard, nails were positioned so they scraped against the board if it bent. The floors made chirping noises like a bird when walked on.

Bodyguards

Some samurai or daimyo hired ninja to protect them from attack. Ninja bodyguards not only stayed close to their employer, but also designed their house or castle to be safe against most of the standard ninja attack methods.

When looking for a ninja bodyguard, Tsugaru Gembin set a test for applicants. They had to be able to steal his pillow while he was sleeping on it and escape undetected. Ninja Shoshunjin applied for the job, but left when he was told of the test. One night a week later it rained. Gembin felt water drip on his head as he slept and sat up to wipe it away. When he put his head back down the pillow had gone! The next morning Shoshunjin knocked at the front gate holding the missing pillow. He got the job!

ANTI-NINJA CASTLE DESIGN

Himeji castle was designed to stop ninja assassin attacks. It was laid out as a gigantic maze made up of 83 buildings and 81 gates linked by long paths that twist, turn and double back. In places the paths were covered with shingle, which crunched when walked on.

The powerful daimyo Oda Nobunaga was betrayed by one of his followers, Akechi Mitsuhide. Nobunaga's loyal samurai Tokugawa Ieyasu met ninja Hattori Hanzo, who offered to get Ieyasu home safely through territory swarming with Mitsuhide's soldiers. Hanzo made him promise to never tell anyone how it was done. Twenty years later, when Ieyasu became shogun, he rewarded Hanzo for his help.

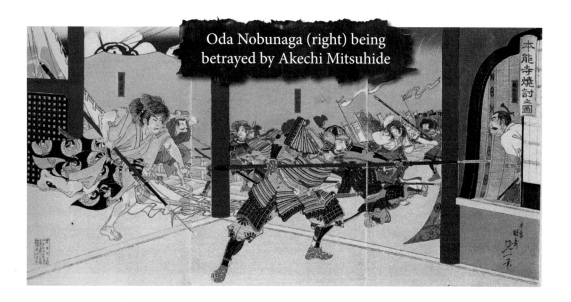
Oda Nobunaga (right) being betrayed by Akechi Mitsuhide

It is said that the shogun Tokugawa Hidetada employed a ninja to design his palace. He wanted it to appear that he welcomed guests with complete trust, when in fact security was very tight. The ninja designed a seating mat with weapons hidden inside it. The chamber where Hidetada met guests had a false paper wall, behind which stood armed guards who could break into the room at any time. Finally, the corridors were fitted with hinged floors that could be collapsed easily to stop attackers escaping down them!

Great ninja

All Ninja were highly skilled at the secret arts of spying, deception and assassination - but a select handful were great masters who were held in awe by all other ninja.

YAMATO TAKERU

Often counted as the first ninja, Yamato Takeru is probably better thought of as one of the first men to use ninja techniques. He was born in about CE 72, son of the Emperor Keiko. He was a bad-tempered man who quarrelled with many nobles and was involved in many fights. He defeated his enemies using cunning and a gift for disguises.

TOMO SUKESADA

In 1560 the ninja Tomo Sukesada was hired by Tokugawa Ieyasu to destroy a castle held by the Imagawa clan. Sukesada led a group of no less than 80 ninja. A small group got into the castle first to discover its layout and work out the best time to attack. Then all 80 ninja crept into the castle before launching a surprise attack that saw the castle burned down, 200 defenders killed and the rest sent fleeing.

HATTORI HANZO

Born in 1542, Hanzo was a ninja thought to have been the greatest spear fighter in Japanese history. He achieved fame when he saved the life of the future shogun Tokugawa Ieyasu. He is said to have had the ability to vanish from one place and instantly appear somewhere else. He retired to become a monk and lived in Edo Castle, where a gate still bears his name.

KAWAI AKI-NO-KAMI

In 1485 shogun Ashikaga Yoshihisa led a large army against Rokkaku Takayori. Yoshihisa led a team of ninja including Kawai Aki-no-kami that went ahead of the main army, to scout out a route or spy on the enemy. He became famous for his ninja skills.

HATTORI MASASHIGE

Masashige was born in 1580 but achieved fame for leading the ninja during the siege of Osaka Castle in 1614. He then became a loyal servant of the Tokugawa Shogunate, organising a number of ninja operations against rebellious nobles and samurai.

ISHIKAWA GOEMON

Goemon was a famous bandit who used ninja techniques to pull off some spectacular robberies and murders. He was born in Iga province in 1558 and brought up as a member of a ninja clan. He left to become a robber. By 1590 he was leading a large gang of bandits who attacked temples, castles and towns using ninja techniques. He was captured in 1594 when trying to attack the samurai warlord Toyotomi Hideyoshi and executed by being boiled alive in an iron pot.

FUMA KOTARO

During the 1580s and 1590s Kotaro led a group of 200 ninja who specialised in sabotage and spying. His greatest exploit came in 1580 when he led his men in a secret night attack on the army of Takeda Katsuyori. The ninja got into the camp without being seen, then attacked the sleeping samurai. Because they were dressed as Katsuyori samurai, the ninja managed to slip away.

That's fearless!

Famous Koga ninja, Sarutobi Sasuke, qualified as master of all the ninja skills when he was still a boy. He was known for his monkey-like agility. He went on his first missions when he was around nine years old.

MOCHIZUKI CHIYOME

Although she was the wife of samurai warlord Mochizuki Nobumasa of Shinano, Chiyome was born into a clan of Kaga ninja. In about 1560 she started recruiting girl orphans into a secret camp where they were trained in ninja skills. Eventually Chiyome had about 200 women ninja, who were sent on missions for her husband's Takeda clan. After her death the female ninja disbanded.

MOMOCHI SANDAYU

Widely recognised to be one of the three greatest ninja ever, Sandayu organised a large number of ninja operations for Japanese noblemen in the 16th century. When the Iga province was conquered by Oda Nobunaga and the ninja clans broken up, Sandayu vanished. Some said he was killed in battle, others that he used his ninja skills to escape, and lived in retirement in Kii province.

FUJIBAYASHI NAGATO

Known only from legends, Nagato was a leader of an Iga ninja clan. His clan entered the service of the Tokugawa shoguns. In 1676 they wrote the book *Bansenshukai*, which is full of information about the ninja.

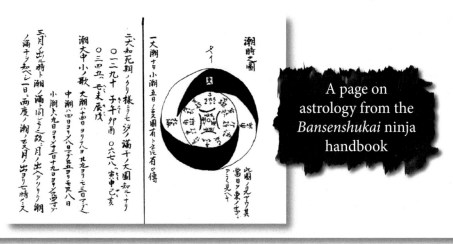

A page on astrology from the *Bansenshukai* ninja handbook

Ninjutsu

Disguises

The arts of **ninjutsu** are the skills and techniques of the ninja. During the years of the Iga and Koga clans, these were kept close secrets by the families and clans of ninja. Later they were taught in schools training ninja for the daimyo and for the shogun. One the most important skills was **hensojutso**, or disguises.

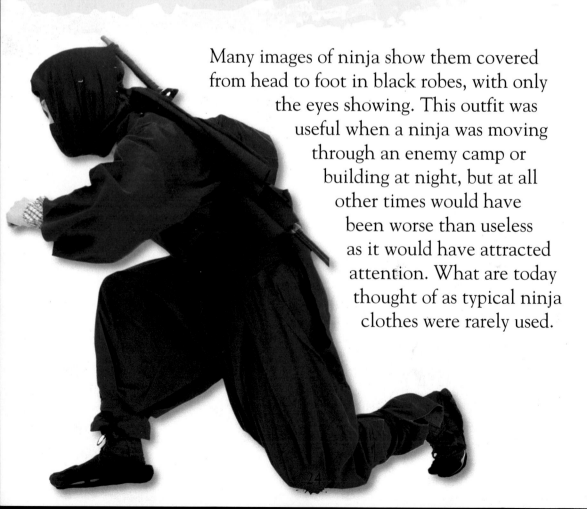

Many images of ninja show them covered from head to foot in black robes, with only the eyes showing. This outfit was useful when a ninja was moving through an enemy camp or building at night, but at all other times would have been worse than useless as it would have attracted attention. What are today thought of as typical ninja clothes were rarely used.

When they knew that they might be tracked by the enemy, ninja used a variety of tricks to hide their tracks. They might tie a branch to their backs so that the leaves dragged behind them and wiped out prints. Some had wooden blocks that fitted on to the undersides of their sandals. The blocks were carved into the shapes of animal feet so that the ninja left behind the tracks of a wolf or bear.

With wooden blocks on their feet carved like bear prints, the ninja could escape without leaving human tracks.

A little like an actor, ninja were trained to study how other people moved. Farmers who had spent their lifetime working bent over in fields walked in a different way from builders who often carried heavy loads, or to priests who spent their days looking around for signs from the heavens. Ninja had to be able to move like the person whose clothes they were wearing as a disguise.

NINJUTSU SCHOOL

Today there are several schools that teach ninjutsu. It is not clear how closely modern ninjutsu training matches that of the oniwaban, but it would be fun to train as a ninja!

Favourite ninja roles

Ninja became skilled at all sorts of trades and occupations. Pretending to be different kinds of people helped them move around the country without drawing attention to themselves.

Woodmen

A favourite ninja disguise was that of a woodman. These workers roamed through the forests and hills rather than staying put in a single town or village. It was easy for the ninja to enter a new area undetected.

Yamabushi

Yamabushi were religious men who often travelled from temple to temple. Yamabushi might live alone in remote areas, or live with a daimyo to offer spiritual advice. Pretending to be a yamabushi was a disguise that allowed a ninja to visit whatever part of Japan he wished.

chain armour

That's fearless!

Ninja would wear clothes such as this old Japanese travel cape and hood. It would disguise the ninja, and make it easy to hide weapons and chain armour under the folds of cloth. They would look harmless, but actually be fearless warriors!

Komuso

The komuso monks were Buddhists that meditated using music. A key element in their religion was to get rid of self-importance, which they did by wearing a wicker basket over their head! The komuso would sit for hours with baskets on their heads while they played a bamboo flute. Pretending to be a komuso was a useful disguise for a ninja.

Sarugaku

Sarugaku actors and musicians would travel around Japan putting on shows. The shows were mostly comedy plays and dancing. A group of ninja would spend weeks travelling putting on shows before they moved to the place where their mission was to take place.

a Japanese actor's mask

Camouflage

Moving without being seen was a key ninja skill. Whether the ninja was collecting information, seeking to escape or plotting an assassination he needed to be able to gain access to private rooms and approach an enemy under cover. Camouflage was often the best way to go.

Some ninja carried with them what were called 'dirty robes'. These were loose clothes that were kept deliberately dirty, and had holes or pockets that the ninja could stuff tufts of grass, branches, leaves and other natural objects into. By quickly putting on the dirty robes and crouching very still a ninja could camouflage themselves.

BREATHING UNDERWATER

Some ninja claimed that they could hide underwater by holding their breath for long periods of time. In fact they were using a **takezutsu**, a hollow bamboo pipe that they kept tucked inside their robes. When they wanted to hide underwater, the ninja would slip beneath the water among some reeds, then poke the takezutsu up so that it resembled a reed, and breathe through it.

A ninja could stay underwater for a long time using a bamboo pipe.

Sometimes ninja would pretend to be underwater. Hattori Hanzo dived into a river while his friend, shogun Tokugawa Ieyasu, was eating a meal on the bank. Hanzo splashed loudly as he dived in. After several hours, Ieyasu decided it was time to leave and called for Hanzo. He came up from the water in the same place! It was a trick. Hanzo had got out of the river. When he was called he swam back underwater to emerge where he had dived in!

Sometimes one group of ninja would do something to attract attention. With everyone watching them, other waiting ninja could complete the real task.

DISTRACTION TECHNIQUES

In 1637 during the siege of Hara Castle, Matsudaira Nobutsuna wanted ninja to get into the castle to find out how much food the **garrison** had. After studying the castle defences for several days, the ninja decided that there was only one way in. They asked Nobutsuna to pretend to attack the castle gateway. The defenders put out their lanterns and rushed to the gateway to defend it. This allowed the ninja to clamber over the castle wall on the far side in darkness without being seen.

A map of the siege of Hara castle

Overcoming obstacles

Getting into places that were heavily guarded and fortified was a key task of the ninja. Whether the ninja was collecting information or killing an enemy, he first had to get into the building. There was a variety of equipment a skilled ninja could use to get to where he needed to be.

Silk ladders

To get up walls that were too smooth to get a grip ninja used a special form of rope ladder. The rungs were made of bamboo, and the ropes of thin silk. The ladder was topped by a pair of iron hooks. Standing at the foot of the wall, the ninja would throw the ladder up so that the hooks caught on the top of the wall.

Bamboo ladders were lightweight and could be rolled up and carried in a small tube.

Hooks

A **kurokagi** was a short, stout iron hook attached to a wooden handle. The hook was strong enough to smash into wooden walls or to find a gap in stone walls. Kurokagi were used in pairs, one in each hand, to help the ninja get a grip when climbing vertical walls. Ninja also used iron claws called hokode to help them climb. They could be used to climb or as a weapon.

One of a pair of mizugumo

Hole carver

A **tsubokiri** was a twin-bladed knife. It could be used to carve a tiny hole in wooden walls. The blades were then eased apart to widen the hole just enough to allow the ninja to peek through and see what was happening beyond.

Long thin saw

A saw called a **hamagari** had specially sharpened, small teeth that could cut through wood in silence. It was used to cut a hole in a wall just large enough for the ninja to wriggle through.

Listening device

The **hikigane** was a hollow wooden tube that flared out at one end. The flared end was put against a wooden door or wall and the narrower end put to the ear. This allowed the ninja to hear any noises being made in the room beyond the door or wall. He could even listen in on private conversations.

Weapons with blades

The ninja valued the skills of the Japanese swordsmiths as much as the samurai did. But while the samurai wanted impressive swords for open warfare, the ninja needed smaller weapons for undercover operations.

Swords

The typical ninja sword was the **ninjato**. This weapon was short, and had a blade that was straight, heavy, and thick. This design made the weapon easier to carry while scaling walls or wriggling under floorboards. It was probably thick and heavy so that it could be used as a multipurpose tool for cutting through bushes or wooden walls as well as for fighting.

Long swords

Many ninja preferred to carry a **katana**, the longer sword usually carried by samurai. This was a highly effective weapon in most situations, being extremely sharp and long. However, such a long weapon was difficult to hide and would need to be carried openly. It was usually carried by being strapped to the back, which kept it out of the way of the hands and legs if the ninja needed to climb or swim to his destination.

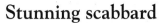

Stunning scabbard

The sword scabbard used by ninja sometimes carried a hidden pouch that contained pepper or iron filings. When the sword was drawn quickly the pouch would burst, sending a spray of its contents forwards toward the opponent. This could temporarily blind the enemy, allowing the ninja to get his blow in first.

sword scabbard

SECRET WEAPON

The **shikomizue** was a specialised form of sword that had a blade similar to that of the katana. Its outward appearance was very different, though. The handle and scabbard were disguised to look like an ordinary object, such as a wooden walking stick or a bamboo pole. The joint between the two was hidden so that it appeared to be one solid object. Only when the ninja twisted it in a certain way did the cover come apart to reveal the secret blade!

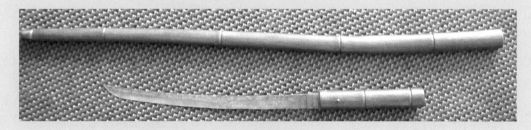

Multipurpose weapons

Ninja needed to be equipped for all sorts of situations. This led them to develop a number of weapons that could be used for different purposes so that the ninja could carry just one item instead of a number of weapons or tools. They also learned how to use everyday tools as deadly weapons so that they could be armed when appearing to be harmless.

Chains

A kusarigama had a short, single-edged blade at the end of a wooden pole or handle. At the other end of the pole was a long iron chain with a heavy iron weight on the end, often with sharp spikes. (There's a picture of one on page 11.) A ninja would whirl the iron chain around his head and fling the weapon. The weight would wrap around the arms or legs of the opponent and the ninja could then attack them with the blade. The small kusarigama could be easily hidden.

CAPTURING THE ENEMY

This weapon was used when the ninja needed to capture a person alive. A **kusari-fundo** was an iron chain that had heavy weights, often handle-shaped, at either end. It was thrown at the victim, wrapping itself around the person and making them unable to flee.

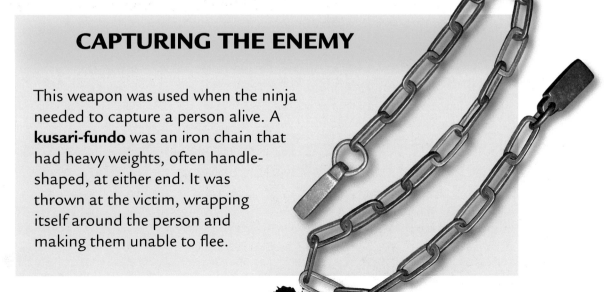

That's fearless!

The **chigiriki** looked like a bamboo staff, but hidden inside was an iron chain and an iron block. With a flick of the wrist the ninja could push out the chain and block, and then whirl the staff around his head. The block could build up enough speed to be able to crush skulls or break bones!

a chigiriki

Multi-tools

The **kyoketsu-shoge** was a heavy, single-edged knife that had a hooked, double-edged blade sticking out close to the hilt. It could be used to stab or slash. The wooden hilt was attached to a long rope woven out of horse or human hair. The blade could be used as a grappling iron for climbing or to slash at a distant opponent who was otherwise out of range. Some examples have an iron ring on the far end of the rope. This may have acted as a weight when the rope was thrown.

Throwing weapons

The small shuriken were throwing weapons that came in a wide variety of shapes and sizes. Although it was not only the ninja who used them, they perfected the design for specialised ninja uses and used them with greater skill than other fighters.

Stars

A **makibishi** was a six- or eight-pointed star of sharp metal spikes. Whichever way up the makibishi landed on the ground, one of the spikes would point upwards. Makibishi would be dropped by the ninja if he were fleeing from enemies. The spikes went through the sandals worn by most Japanese men and slowed down pursuers.

Throwing knife

The **tanto-gata** knife had a double-edged blade. It was designed to slide from the fingers when thrown. Its blade would point forward in flight until it hit the target. There were two forms of tanto-gata. One had a very thin blade and was used against unprotected targets, the other had a thick blade and could penetrate armour.

Throwing stars

The hira-shuriken came in a variety of shapes, but all were small and flat with a sharpened outer edge and a hole in the middle. They were thrown so that they spun in the air. This way of throwing meant they could be thrown a great distance. Shuriken were often used to distract an enemy rather than kill them.

That's fearless!

Shuriken could be used like a makibishi, injuring those who stepped on them, or wrapped and either lit to cause fire, or soaked in poison and lit to create poisonous smoke. They could also be used as a weapon in close combat. Coated with poison, they could be deadly if either thrown or left for a curious victim to pick up.

Bo-shuriken are straight, metal dart-like spikes that could be thrown at the enemy.

bo-shuriken

THE INVISIBLE SWORDSMAN

Some ninja claimed that when they went into action they took with them another ninja who was totally invisible and who carried a sword. Enemy soldiers facing such a ninja would experience blows to their armour or cuts to exposed parts of their body while still some distance away. Naturally they turned to hunt the invisible swordsman. In reality the blows had been inflicted by shuriken!

Magical weapons

The ninja claimed that they had many magical powers. They could talk to animals, turn themselves into animals, or make themselves invisible. These magical skills allowed the ninja to carry out their tasks and frighten their opponents.

Japanese holy men used ritual hand movements to symbolise gods and spirits. When performed properly the hand movements, known as **kuji kiri**, allowed the spirit to enter the human world for a short period of time to do the bidding of the holy man, perhaps to heal a sick person. Ninja used similar kuji kiri primarily as aids to mental or physical concentration.

The Nine Kuji
The traditional nine kuji used by ninja were:

Rin - Power

Sha - Healing

Retsu - Dimension

Pyo - Energy

Kai - Intuition

Zai - Creation

Toh - Harmony

Jin - Awareness

Zen - Absolute

NIKKI DANJO

Nikki Danjo was a ninja said to have lived in the 1660s. It is unclear how many of the stories about him are true. He was said to use kuji kiri to transform himself into a rat. He then gained access to buildings and fortresses to steal objects or overhear conversations. He also used kuji kiri to walk on clouds. Nikki Danjo is a popular villain in Japanese theatre.

Onibi no jutsu is a magical power that allowed the ninja to control fire, sending flames toward the enemy or causing explosions to take place at a distance. In fact, the ninja were probably using fireworks and exploding grenades, combined with distraction tactics. One ninja would stand in the moonlight and perform kuji kiri, while another ninja moved silently around in the shadows lighting fireworks and throwing them in time with the other ninja's hand movements.

That's fearless!

Ninja would sometimes place flammable liquid and explosive powder in the mouth and nostrils of wooden demon masks. The ninja would then wear the mask and set the fire effects going so that he appeared to be breathing smoke and flames!

Ninja timeline

The ninja were active in Japan for centuries, but the great secrecy under which they operated means that it is not always easy to know what they were doing, when they were doing it, or who they were doing it to. Here are some of the secret ninja dates that did get recorded. The 'c' stands for 'circa', which means 'around'.

1000

• **c.90**
Imperial prince Yamato Takeru uses ninja-like tactics in his various feuds. On one famous occasion he dresses as an attractive woman to get close to an enemy and kill him.

500

CE

• **932**
The spy Kharumaru is executed after using ninja-like techniques to spy on his own employer, the warlord Taira no Masakado.

Yamato Takeru dressed as a maidservant, preparing to kill the Kumaso leaders

c.1335
Career begins of Kumawaka, who used ninja tactics to gain revenge for the death of his father.

c.1400
The Iga and Koga ninja clans are first recorded as hiring themselves out to perform activities on behalf of samurai warlords.

c.1380
The chronicle Taiheiki records a history of the 14th century civil war in the reign of the Emperor Go-Daigo. It contains the earliest references to ninja and their exploits.

1541
A team of ninja secretly enter Kasagi castle and set it on fire.

1500

Emperor Go-Daigo

1558
A team of 48 ninja are hired by samurai warlord Rokkaku Yoshitaka to set fire to Sawayama castle. They enter the castle by carrying lanterns decorated with the badge of the castle commanders.

- **1560**
  A team of 80 ninja enter and destroy a castle held by the Imagawa clan. This is one of the few times on record that ninja led a major military campaign on their own.

- **1561**
  Kizawa Nagamasa hires three Iga ninja to infiltrate a fortress in Maibara. After a dispute over tactics, Nagamasa backs down and allows the ninja to operate as they see fit.

- **1600**
  Samurai Ie Naomasa is wounded at the Battle of Sekigahara, but his life is saved by medicine administered by a ninja.

1550

1600

- **1581**
  A rare failure for the ninja occurs when three ninja open fire on Oda Nobunaga. They kill seven men standing close to Nobunaga, but the warlord himself escapes!

- **1578**
  Samurai daimyo Uesugi Kenshin is assassinated by a ninja who stabs him as he goes to the bathroom.

A statue of Oda Nobunaga

The squeaky nails in a nightingale floor

- **1626**
  Nijo castle is completed for Shogun Tukugawa Iemitsu with extensive 'nightingale floors' to act as an alarm against ninja attacks.

1700

- **c.1730**
  Shogun Tokugawa Yoshimune forms an elite guard of ninja called the oniwaban. He uses them to spy on nobles and to guard against a rebellion.

1800

- **1649**
  Shogun Tokugawa Iemitsu passes a law forbidding junior daimyo from employing ninja for any reason at all.

- **1868**
  The oniwaban are disbanded. It is the end of the ninja, although ninja techniques continue to be used and taught.

- **1675**
  Publication of the book *Bansenshukai*, which is a training manual for ninja.

What Do You Know?

Can you answer these questions about the Ninja?

1. What did the ninja call themselves?

2. In which two regions of Japan did the early ninja live?

3. What did the ninja 'black potion' do?

4. When were the oniwaban abolished?

5. How did Kirigakure Saizo overhear his target's conversations?

6. What is a nightingale floorboard?

7. How were ninja usually paid?

8. What is sabotage?

9. Did ninja always wear black robes?

10. How did ninja hide underwater for hours at a time?

Answers on page 48

Further Information

Books

Malam, John. *Avoid Being a Ninja Warrior!* (The Danger Zone). Brighton, UK: Salariya, 2012.

Turnbull, Stephen. *Ninja AD 1460-1650*. Oxford, UK: Osprey Publishing, 2003.

Turnbull, Stephen. *Tokugawa Ieyasu*. Oxford, UK: Osprey Publishing, 2012.

Websites

A site full of ninja history, stories, and fun facts
http://www.winjutsu.com/ninjakids/

Kids Web Japan, information on Japan, and the ninja
http://web-japan.org/kidsweb/explore/history/index.html

A guide to the ninja in Japan
http://www.japan-guide.com/e/e2295.html

Every effort has been made by the publisher to ensure that these websites contain no inappropriate or offensive material. However, because of the nature of the Internet, it is impossible to guarantee that the content of these sites will not be altered. We strongly advise that Internet access is supervised by a responsible adult.

Glossary

assassins People who murder a politically important person either for pay or from loyalty to a cause.

astrology The supposed ability to tell the future by studying the movements of the stars.

chigiriki A bamboo pole containing a hidden weapon.

chunin A senior ninja who organised missions.

civil war A war between opposing groups of citizens of the same country or nation.

daimyo A land-owning lord of Japan.

garrison A military post.

genin A junior ninja who carried out missions.

hamagari A saw used to cut a gap in a wall.

hensojutso The ninja art of disguise.

hikigane A listening device to hear what is taking place on the other side of a wall.

jonin The leader of a ninja clan.

katana A long, curved sword used by samurai.

kuji kiri The alleged ability of some ninja to use magic by waving the hands.

kurokagi An iron hook used for climbing walls.

kusari-fundo A chain with weights at each end used as a weapon.

kusarigama A weapon with a short, single-edged blade mounted on a wooden pole.

kyoketsu-shoge A knife which had a second blade sticking out close to the hilt.

makibishi A weapon designed to slow pursuers by injuring their feet.

mizugumo Inflatable shoes of wood and leather used to walk over water.

naginata A bladed weapon on the end of a pole.

ninjato A sword with a short, straight blade.

ninjutsu The art of training to be a ninja.

onibi no jutsu The art of using fireworks to terrify the enemy.

samurai The warrior class of Japan until 1878. The samurai had important legal and social privileges.

shikomizue A concealed sword disguised as a cane or walking stick.

shinobi Another name for ninja.

shogunate A government controlled by shoguns.

shoguns Originally senior military commanders, but later men who ruled Japan on behalf of the emperor.

shuriken Any weapon that was thrown by hand.

takezutsu A hollow bamboo pipe that ninja could use to breathe underwater.

tanto-gata A throwing knife.

tributes Payments in money or objects made by one ruler to another as a form of tax.

tsubokiri A knife used to cut a hole in a wall.

warlords Military leaders who govern an area by force.

Index

Answers to Quiz

1. shinobi
2. Iga and Koga
3. it stopped bleeding from wounds
4. 1868
5. by squirming silently from room to room under the floorboards
6. a floorboard designed to squeak loudly when someone walks on it
7. with sacks of rice
8. the act of entering enemy territory in order to destroy supplies, weapons, etc.
9. no, they wore them only when working at night
10. by breathing through a hollow reed